IMPRIMI POTEST
Bradley M. Schaeffer, S.J.

NIHIL OBSTAT
Rev. Robert Coerver
Censor Liborum

IMPRIMATUR
† Most Rev. Charles V. Grahmann
Bishop of Dallas

December 23, 1991

The *Nihil Obstat* and *Imprimatur* are official declarations that the work contains nothing contrary to Faith and Morals. It is not implied thereby that those granting the *Nihil Obstat* and *Imprimatur* agree with the contents, statements, or opinions expressed.

ACKNOWLEDGMENT

Unless otherwise noted, all Scripture quotations are from the *Good News Bible,* in Today's English Version. Copyright © American Bible Society 1966, 1971, 1976. Used by permission.

Send all inquiries to:
Tabor Publishing
200 East Bethany Drive
Allen, Texas 75002-3804

ISBN 0-7829-0103-4

    4 5 6 7   97 96 95 94

VISION 2000

Praying Scripture in a Contemporary Way

Mark Link, S.J.

A
Cycle

TABOR
PUBLISHING

Allen, Texas